DIARY 2009

F
FRANCES LINCOLN LIMITED
PUBLISHERS

Frances Lincoln Limited
4 Torriano Mews
Torriano Avenue
London NW5 2RZ
www.franceslincoln.com

National Railway Museum Diary 2009
Copyright © Frances Lincoln Limited 2008
This product is produced under licence from NMSI
Trading Limited (the wholly owned subsidiary of The
Board of Trustees of the Science Museum). Licence no.
0181. Text © NMSI Trading Ltd. Images © NRM/Science
and Society Picture Library, London. The National
Railway Museum Collection is a registered trademark
No. 2309517. Royalties from the sale of this diary help
fund and support the NRM, York.
To buy prints of the images in this diary see
www.ssplprints.com

Astronomical information © Crown Copyright.
Reproduced by permission of the Controller of Her
Majesty's Stationery Office and the UK Hydrographic
Office (www.ukho.gov.uk)

British Library cataloguing-in-publication data
A catalogue record for this book is available from the
British Library

ISBN: 978-0-7112-2839-9

FRONT COVER: 'The Queen of Scots', Pullman Company
poster, 1923–4. Poster produced to promote the pullman
service between Glasgow/Edinburgh and London. Artwork
by Septimus E Scott (1879–1965).

BACK COVER: Schoolboy train-spotters at Newcastle
Station, Tyne & Wear, August 1950.

TITLE PAGE: 'A Century of Progress', LMS centenary
poster, 1938. Poster produced for the London, Midland &
Scottish Railway (LMS) to promote celebrations at
London's Euston Station to mark the centenary of the
London & Birmingham Railway.

INTRODUCTION: 'Cornish Riviera Express' GWR steam
locomotive no 4062, c.1904. Painted photograph by F
Moore showing the Great Western Railway's (GWR)
Cornish Riviera Express locomotive, which entered service
in 1904, on what was at the time the world's longest non-
stop run. The train ran daily, non-stop express services
from Paddington, London, to Plymouth, Devon, with a
journey time of 265 minutes. For over twenty years it held
the world record for the longest non-stop run, and was
also unique in carrying three slip portions detached at
speed at Westbury, Taunton and Exeter.
*All double-page images and detail images are captioned on
the final page of the diary.*

ABOUT THE NATIONAL RAILWAY MUSEUM

The National Railway Museum is the largest railway
museum in the world. Its permanent displays and
collections are the most comprehensive and
significant in their field, illustrating the history of the
British railways and railway engineering from the
industrial revolution to the present day. You'll find
many examples of world railway history, including
Queen Victoria's favourite carriage and Japanese
Bullet trains. Since first opening in 1975 the museum's
unique blend of education and entertainment has
thrilled 20 million visitors, young and old.

In addition to the collection, the National Railway
Museum contains a valuable archive which includes a
fabulous collection of advertising posters charting the
history of rail, a vast selection of railway memorabilia
including railway passes and uniforms and fabrics and
furniture from the famous Royal Carriages.

The recently opened Search Engine library and archive
centre allows visitors access to railway books,
magazines and other archive materials as well as
providing help with railway related questions. For
more information visit www.nrm.org.uk

National Railway Museum
Leeman Road
York, YO26 4XJ

Telephone:	08448 153 139
Fax:	08448 153 404
e-mail:	nrm@nrm.org.uk
website:	www.nrm.org.uk

24 hour recorded information line: 08448 153 139

Admission free

Open
Daily: 10 am to 6 pm
Closed: 24th, 25th & 26th December

Disabled visitors
Ramps and lifts provide access to most parts of the
museum and wheelchairs may be borrowed from the
entrance. There are free disabled parking bays outside
the City Entrance. Support dogs are welcome.

JANUARY

M	T	W	T	F	S	S
			1	2	3	4
5	6	7	8	9	10	11
12	13	14	15	16	17	18
19	20	21	22	23	24	25
26	27	28	29	30	31	

FEBRUARY

M	T	W	T	F	S	S
						1
2	3	4	5	6	7	8
9	10	11	12	13	14	15
16	17	18	19	20	21	22
23	24	25	26	27	28	

MARCH

M	T	W	T	F	S	S
						1
2	3	4	5	6	7	8
9	10	11	12	13	14	15
16	17	18	19	20	21	22
23	24	25	26	27	28	29
30	31					

APRIL

M	T	W	T	F	S	S
		1	2	3	4	5
6	7	8	9	10	11	12
13	14	15	16	17	18	19
20	21	22	23	24	25	26
27	28	29	30			

MAY

M	T	W	T	F	S	S
				1	2	3
4	5	6	7	8	9	10
11	12	13	14	15	16	17
18	19	20	21	22	23	24
25	26	27	28	29	30	31

JUNE

M	T	W	T	F	S	S
1	2	3	4	5	6	7
8	9	10	11	12	13	14
15	16	17	18	19	20	21
22	23	24	25	26	27	28
29	30					

JULY

M	T	W	T	F	S	S
		1	2	3	4	5
6	7	8	9	10	11	12
13	14	15	16	17	18	19
20	21	22	23	24	25	26
27	28	29	30	31		

AUGUST

M	T	W	T	F	S	S
					1	2
3	4	5	6	7	8	9
10	11	12	13	14	15	16
17	18	19	20	21	22	23
24	25	26	27	28	29	30
31						

SEPTEMBER

M	T	W	T	F	S	S
	1	2	3	4	5	6
7	8	9	10	11	12	13
14	15	16	17	18	19	20
21	22	23	24	25	26	27
28	29	30				

OCTOBER

M	T	W	T	F	S	S
			1	2	3	4
5	6	7	8	9	10	11
12	13	14	15	16	17	18
19	20	21	22	23	24	25
26	27	28	29	30	31	

NOVEMBER

M	T	W	T	F	S	S
						1
2	3	4	5	6	7	8
9	10	11	12	13	14	15
16	17	18	19	20	21	22
23	24	25	26	27	28	29
30						

DECEMBER

M	T	W	T	F	S	S
	1	2	3	4	5	6
7	8	9	10	11	12	13
14	15	16	17	18	19	20
21	22	23	24	25	26	27
28	29	30	31			

JANUARY

M	T	W	T	F	S	S
				1	2	3
4	5	6	7	8	9	10
11	12	13	14	15	16	17
18	19	20	21	22	23	24
25	26	27	28	29	30	31

FEBRUARY

M	T	W	T	F	S	S
1	2	3	4	5	6	7
8	9	10	11	12	13	14
15	16	17	18	19	20	21
22	23	24	25	26	27	28

MARCH

M	T	W	T	F	S	S
1	2	3	4	5	6	7
8	9	10	11	12	13	14
15	16	17	18	19	20	21
22	23	24	25	26	27	28
29	30	31				

APRIL

M	T	W	T	F	S	S
			1	2	3	4
5	6	7	8	9	10	11
12	13	14	15	16	17	18
19	20	21	22	23	24	25
26	27	28	29	30		

MAY

M	T	W	T	F	S	S
					1	2
3	4	5	6	7	8	9
10	11	12	13	14	15	16
17	18	19	20	21	22	23
24	25	26	27	28	29	30
31						

JUNE

M	T	W	T	F	S	S
	1	2	3	4	5	6
7	8	9	10	11	12	13
14	15	16	17	18	19	20
21	22	23	24	25	26	27
28	29	30				

JULY

M	T	W	T	F	S	S
			1	2	3	4
5	6	7	8	9	10	11
12	13	14	15	16	17	18
19	20	21	22	23	24	25
26	27	28	29	30	31	

AUGUST

M	T	W	T	F	S	S
						1
2	3	4	5	6	7	8
9	10	11	12	13	14	15
16	17	18	19	20	21	22
23	24	25	26	27	28	29
30	31					

SEPTEMBER

M	T	W	T	F	S	S
		1	2	3	4	5
6	7	8	9	10	11	12
13	14	15	16	17	18	19
20	21	22	23	24	25	26
27	28	29	30			

OCTOBER

M	T	W	T	F	S	S
				1	2	3
4	5	6	7	8	9	10
11	12	13	14	15	16	17
18	19	20	21	22	23	24
25	26	27	28	29	30	31

NOVEMBER

M	T	W	T	F	S	S
1	2	3	4	5	6	7
8	9	10	11	12	13	14
15	16	17	18	19	20	21
22	23	24	25	26	27	28
29	30					

DECEMBER

M	T	W	T	F	S	S
		1	2	3	4	5
6	7	8	9	10	11	12
13	14	15	16	17	18	19
20	21	22	23	24	25	26
27	28	29	30	31		

INTRODUCTION

There can be very few people over the last 175 years who have not had their lives transformed in some way by the railways and by the development of rail travel. The rapid technological advances which affected the locomotives and trains themselves would pave the way for great social change. For many, change came in the form of employment as well as a means of travel, whether for pleasure or necessity. The *National Railway Museum Diary 2009* offers a glimpse of this changing world and the people that were a part of it, through selected photographs and illustrations from the National Railway Museum archive.

Documenting the origin and growth of the railways to the present day, the archive collections of the National Railway Museum contain more than a million negatives from official and private sources, along with paintings,

lithographs and engravings of important events in railway history. Notable among the photographs are the 10,000 pictures, both in colour and black and white, which were taken by the British Transport Films Unit from the 1940s to the 1970s that document life and work in Britain. The archive also includes an amazing collection of advertising posters charting the history of rail, the largest collection of railway posters in the world. Commissioned by British Rail and its predecessors the archive includes work by some of Europe's leading graphic artists, including Cassandre, Edward McKnight Kauffer, Fred Taylor and Tom Purvis.

We have brought together a selection of images across these different media to illustrate the development of society and travel from the advent of steam to the 1950s.

DECEMBER • JANUARY

29 MONDAY

30 TUESDAY

31 WEDNESDAY
New Year's Eve

1 THURSDAY
New Year's Day
Holiday, UK, Republic of Ireland, Canada, USA,
Australia and New Zealand

2 FRIDAY
Holiday, Scotland and New Zealand

3 SATURDAY

4 SUNDAY
FIRST QUARTER

'Pleasure. One Way to Pleasure – By Motor-Bus', poster, 1921
Poster advertising travel by motor-bus, showing a group of gypsies singing and dancing. The first motor bus ran in London in 1899, but due to problems of reliability, bus services did not become successful in the city until around 1910. By the 1920s innovations such as pneumatic tyres and covered tops led to improved passenger comfort and enabled buses to overtake trams as the principal means of overland public transport in London. Artwork by C R W Nevinson (1889–1946).

PLEASURE.
ONE WAY TO PLEASURE
– BY MOTOR-BUS

C·R·W·NEVINSON

75 · (500 · 17-2-21)   THE AVENUE PRESS (L. Upcott Gill & Son, Ltd.), 55-57, Drury Lane, London, W.C.2.

JANUARY

5   MONDAY

6   TUESDAY
Epiphany

7   WEDNESDAY

8   THURSDAY

9   FRIDAY

10 SATURDAY

11 SUNDAY
FULL MOON

JANUARY

12 MONDAY

13 TUESDAY

14 WEDNESDAY

15 THURSDAY

16 FRIDAY

17 SATURDAY

18 SUNDAY
LAST QUARTER

JANUARY

19 MONDAY
Holiday, USA (Martin Luther King's Birthday)

20 TUESDAY

21 WEDNESDAY

22 THURSDAY

23 FRIDAY

24 SATURDAY

25 SUNDAY

Peterborough market place, BR poster, 1950–59
British Railways poster (Eastern Region). Artwork by Bertram Prance.

BERTRAM PRANCE

PETERBOROUGH

SEE ENGLAND BY RAIL

PUBLISHED BY THE RAILWAY EXECUTIVE (EASTERN REGION) (PP 1122)   PRINTED IN GREAT BRITAIN   CHORLEY & PICKERSGILL LTD   LEEDS

FEBRUARY

---

9 MONDAY
FULL MOON

---

10 TUESDAY

---

11 WEDNESDAY

---

12 THURSDAY
Holiday, USA (Lincoln's Birthday)

---

13 FRIDAY

---

14 SATURDAY
St. Valentine's Day

---

15 SUNDAY

Goodbye kiss for a soldier, 21st May 1940
A soldier hoists his sweetheart over the railings at a London railway station to kiss her goodbye before leaving to join the
British Expeditionary Force in France.

FEBRUARY

2 MONDAY
FIRST QUARTER

3 TUESDAY

4 WEDNESDAY

5 THURSDAY

6 FRIDAY
Holiday, New Zealand (Waitangi Day)
Accession of Queen Elizabeth II

7 SATURDAY

8 SUNDAY

JANUARY · FEBRUARY

---

26 MONDAY
NEW MOON
Chinese New Year
Holiday, Australia (Australia Day)

---

27 TUESDAY

---

28 WEDNESDAY

---

29 THURSDAY

---

30 FRIDAY

---

31 SATURDAY

---

1 SUNDAY

FEBRUARY

16 MONDAY
LAST QUARTER
Holiday, USA (Washington's Birthday)

17 TUESDAY

18 WEDNESDAY
Some time ago recd message 'You owe £22.50' to Bclays. So had the Bank clerk tryg to find out to whom. We decided to destroy our Bclay cards wh. is a pity as it's a long way to Santander. Stephen arr'd early this morng & gave me god advice on banks

19 THURSDAY

20 FRIDAY

21 SATURDAY

22 SUNDAY

'Winter Sports – Go by Train', BR poster, 1965
British Railways poster (Southern Region). Artwork by John Court.

FEBRUARY · MARCH

23 MONDAY

24 TUESDAY
Shrove Tuesday

25 WEDNESDAY
NEW MOON
Ash Wednesday

26 THURSDAY

27 FRIDAY

28 SATURDAY

1 SUNDAY
St. David's Day

**'Have Your Tickets Ready' (detail), GWR/LMS/LNER/SR/LT
poster, 1940s**
Poster produced for Great Western Railway (GWR), London,
Midland & Scottish Railway (LMS), London & North Eastern
Railway (LNER), Southern Railway (SR) and London Transport
to remind passengers to have their tickets ready to present to
the ticket inspectors. Artwork by Reginald Mayes (1900–92).

KENT - THE GA

SEE BRITAIN

RDEN OF ENGLAND
BY TRAIN

MARCH

---

2   MONDAY

---

3   TUESDAY

---

4   WEDNESDAY
FIRST QUARTER

---

5   THURSDAY

---

6   FRIDAY

---

7   SATURDAY

---

8   SUNDAY

Air passenger weighing in before a flight, 29th November 1934
Checking-in at Croydon Aerodrome for a flight on the Railway Air Services Ltd's London to Scotland route. In the early days of passenger aviation, the margins between success and failure at take-off were so tight that passengers themselves had to be weighed as well as their luggage.

MARCH

---

9 MONDAY
Commonwealth Day

---

10 TUESDAY

---

11 WEDNESDAY
FULL MOON

---

12 THURSDAY

---

13 FRIDAY

---

14 SATURDAY

---

15 SUNDAY

'The Enchanting River Dart', BR poster, 1961
Poster produced for British Railways (BR) Western Region to promote rail services to Devon. The poster shows a view over the 'enchanting' River Dart. Artwork by Cecil King.

The enchanting
RIVER DART
Travel by Rail to Totnes or Dartmouth
Thence by River Dart Company's Steamers
WESTERN REGION
WRITE TO PUBLICITY MANAGER, THE RIVER DART STEAMBOAT CO. LTD., EMBANKMENT HOUSE, DARTMOUTH, DEVON, FOR BOOKLET DESCRIBING STEAMER TRIPS (MAY-SEPTEMBER)

MARCH

---

16 MONDAY

---

17 TUESDAY
St. Patrick's Day
Holiday, Northern Ireland and Republic of Ireland

---

18 WEDNESDAY
LAST QUARTER

---

19 THURSDAY

20 FRIDAY
Vernal Equinox

---

21 SATURDAY

---

22 SUNDAY
Mothering Sunday, UK

MARCH

---

23 MONDAY

---

24 TUESDAY

---

25 WEDNESDAY

---

26 THURSDAY

NEW MOON

---

27 FRIDAY

---

28 SATURDAY

---

29 SUNDAY

British Summer Time begins

BATH -

INFORMATION FROM SPA DI

TRAVEL BY

PUBLISHED BY THE RAILWAY EXECUTIVE (WESTERN REGION) (P.W.88)

e Georgian City

TOR, THE PUMP ROOM, BATH

RAIN

PRINTED IN GREAT BRITAIN BY JOHNSON AND CO. LTD, LONDON AND MIDDLESBROUGH

MARCH · APRIL

30 MONDAY

31 TUESDAY

1 WEDNESDAY

2 THURSDAY
FIRST QUARTER

3 FRIDAY

4 SATURDAY

5 SUNDAY
Palm Sunday

APRIL

---

6 MONDAY

---

7 TUESDAY

---

8 WEDNESDAY

---

9 THURSDAY

FULL MOON
Maundy Thursday,
Passover (Pesach), First Day

---

10 FRIDAY

Good Friday
Holiday, UK, Canada, USA, Australia and New Zealand

---

11 SATURDAY

---

12 SUNDAY

Easter Day

APRIL

13 MONDAY
Easter Monday Holiday, UK (exc Scotland), Republic of
Ireland, Canada, Australia and New Zealand

14 TUESDAY

15 WEDNESDAY
Passover (Pesach), Seventh Day

16 THURSDAY
Passover (Pesach), Eighth Day

17 FRIDAY
LAST QUARTER

18 SATURDAY

19 SUNDAY

Midland Railway porters unloading milk at Somers Town dock, *c.*1890
Midland Railway porters unloading milk at Somers Town fish and milk dock alongside St Pancras station, London. The churns had a capacity of 17
gallons and were stored in ventilated wagons. The railways precipitated a major shift in the urban diet and by the 1890s they were supplying
about 50 million gallons of milk to London alone.

CHEMINS DE FER DE L'ÉTAT & SOUTHERN RAILWAY

PARIS
St LAZARE

VISITEZ
l'ANGLETERRE

LONDRES

M DÉCHAUX _Imp. Paris.

APRIL

20 MONDAY

21 TUESDAY
Birthday of Queen Elizabeth II

22 WEDNESDAY

23 THURSDAY
St. George's Day

24 FRIDAY

25 SATURDAY
NEW MOON
Holiday, Australia and New Zealand (Anzac Day)

26 SUNDAY

'Visitez l'Angleterre', (Visit England), SR poster, 1932
Poster produced for Southern Railway (SR) for advertising in France. The poster was produced to promote travel from France to England on Southern Railway services. Artwork by Maurice Toussaint.

APRIL • MAY

27 MONDAY

28 TUESDAY

29 WEDNESDAY

30 THURSDAY

1 FRIDAY

FIRST QUARTER

2 SATURDAY

3 SUNDAY

MAY

---

4   MONDAY
Early Spring Bank Holiday, UK and Republic of Ireland

---

5   TUESDAY

---

6   WEDNESDAY

---

7   THURSDAY

---

8   FRIDAY

---

9   SATURDAY
FULL MOON

---

10   SUNDAY
Mother's Day, USA, Canada, Australia and New Zealand

MAY

11 MONDAY

12 TUESDAY

13 WEDNESDAY

14 THURSDAY

15 FRIDAY

16 SATURDAY

17 SUNDAY
LAST QUARTER

'Leicestershire', BR poster, 1950s
Poster produced for British Railways (BR) to promote rail travel to Leicestershire. Artwork by John Bee.

LEICESTERSHIRE

SEE ENGLAND BY RAIL

PUBLISHED BY THE RAILWAY EXECUTIVE (EASTERN REGION) (AB 1040)   PRINTED IN GREAT BRITAIN   JORDISON & CO., LTD., LONDON & MIDDLESBROUGH

MAY

---

18 MONDAY
Holiday, Canada (Victoria Day)

---

19 TUESDAY

---

20 WEDNESDAY

---

21 THURSDAY
Ascension Day

---

22 FRIDAY

---

23 SATURDAY

---

24 SUNDAY
NEW MOON

Carriage cleaners, *c.*1916
Women carriage cleaners on the London & South Western Railway. Women began to be employed on the railways in large numbers during the First World War, replacing men who had joined the armed services.

High Force, Middleton-in-Teesdale

TEESDALE

SEE BRITAIN BY TRAIN

PUBLISHED BY BRITISH RAILWAYS (NORTH EASTERN REGION)   P/65   PRINTED IN GREAT BRITAIN BY STAFFORD & CO., LTD., NETHERFIELD, NOTTINGHAM.

MAY

25 MONDAY
Spring Bank Holiday, UK
Holiday, USA (Memorial Day)

26 TUESDAY

27 WEDNESDAY

28 THURSDAY

29 FRIDAY
Feast of Weeks (Shavuot)

30 SATURDAY

31 SUNDAY
FIRST QUARTER
Whit Sunday (Pentecost)

'Teesdale', BR poster, 1962
Poster produced for British Railways (BR) to promote rail travel to Teesdale, Durham. The poster shows a view of the 70 foot (21 metre) High Force waterfall at Middleton-in-Teesdale. Artwork by Edward Wesson (1910–83).

YORK

SEE BRITAI

BLISHED BY BRITISH RAILWAYS (N.E. REGION)

SHIRE
BY TRAIN

BRITISH RAILWAYS

STAFFORD & CO., LTD., NETHERFIELD, NOTTINGH

JUNE

1   MONDAY
Holiday, Republic of Ireland
Holiday, New Zealand (Queen's Birthday)

2   TUESDAY
Coronation Day

3   WEDNESDAY

4   THURSDAY

5   FRIDAY

6   SATURDAY

7   SUNDAY
FULL MOON
Trinity Sunday

Changing points, *c.*1955
Worker using a Ground Frame on the Kent & East Sussex Railway, by J G Click. This device was used to change points at little-used junctions, a long way from the signal box. The railway was built in 1896 from Robertsbridge to Tenterden, under the name Rother Valley Railway. By the 1950s the railway was no longer making a profit and finally closed to all traffic in 1961. However, it has since been preserved and re-opened.

JUNE

8   MONDAY

9   TUESDAY

10 WEDNESDAY

11 THURSDAY
Corpus Christi

12 FRIDAY

13 SATURDAY
The Queen's Official Birthday

14 SUNDAY

'Ascot Races', GWR poster, 1897
Poster produced for the Great Western Railway (GWR), promoting rail travel from Paddington, London to Windsor Station, showing race-goers in horse-drawn carriages being transported to the Ascot horse races, which were held from the 15th to the 18th of June, 1897. Windsor Castle is seen in the background.

JUNE

15 MONDAY
LAST QUARTER
St. Swithin's Day

16 TUESDAY

17 WEDNESDAY

18 THURSDAY

19 FRIDAY

20 SATURDAY

21 SUNDAY
Summer Solstice
Father's Day, UK, Canada and USA

JUNE

22 MONDAY
NEW MOON

23 TUESDAY

24 WEDNESDAY

25 THURSDAY

26 FRIDAY

27 SATURDAY

28 SUNDAY

Gyrth Russell

JUNE · JULY

29 MONDAY
FIRST QUARTER

30 TUESDAY

1   WEDNESDAY
Holiday, Canada (Canada Day)

2   THURSDAY

3   FRIDAY
Holiday, USA (Independence Day)

4   SATURDAY
Independence Day, USA

5   SUNDAY

Crowds waiting to board trains for their holidays, Waterloo station, London, 26th July 1936

JULY

6 MONDAY

7 TUESDAY
FULL MOON

8 WEDNESDAY

9 THURSDAY

Be budget-wise!
buy a
**SHOPPING
TICKET
TO LONDON**

Wednesdays & Thursdays
any train after 9.30
leave London by 4.30

10 FRIDAY

11 SATURDAY

12 SUNDAY

JULY

13 MONDAY
Battle of the Boyne
Holiday, Northern Ireland

14 TUESDAY

15 WEDNESDAY
LAST QUARTER

16 THURSDAY

17 FRIDAY

18 SATURDAY

19 SUNDAY

DOVERCOURT BAY
HOLIDAY LIDO
(ASSOCIATED WITH BUTLIN'S)
IT'S QUICKER BY RAIL
ILLUSTRATED BOOKLET FREE FROM R.P.SECRETARY HOLIDAY LIDO DOVERCOURT BAY OR ANY L·N·E·R OFFICE OR AGENCY

PUBLISHED BY THE LONDON & NORTH EASTERN RAILWAY.   Printed in England   VINCENT BROOKS, DAY & SON, LTD. LITH. LONDON. W.C.2

JULY

---

20 MONDAY

---

21 TUESDAY

---

22 WEDNESDAY
NEW MOON

---

23 THURSDAY

---

24 FRIDAY

---

25 SATURDAY

---

26 SUNDAY

'Dovercourt Bay, Holiday Lido', LNER poster, 1941
Poster produced for the London & North Eastern Railway (LNER) to promote holiday rail travel to Dovercourt Bay, Essex in association with Butlin's
holiday camps. Artwork by Daphne Padden.

27 MONDAY

28 TUESDAY
FIRST QUARTER

29 WEDNESDAY

30 THURSDAY

31 FRIDAY

1 SATURDAY

2 SUNDAY

'Tynemouth', LNER poster, 1926
Poster produced for the London & North Eastern Railway (LNER) to promote rail services to the coastal town of Tynemouth, Tyne and Wear. This poster was produced just before the General Strike in 1926. Economically, this was a bad year for the railways, especially the LNER. It was said afterwards that the publicity of 1926 had been the only bright feature for the railway. Artwork by Alfred Lambert (1902–70).

SOUT

Cheap fares to S

LIVERPOOL OV

'THE MOST IN

PORT

port daily by the

HEAD RAILWAY

STING ROUTE"

AUGUST

3   MONDAY
Summer Bank Holiday, Scotland
Holiday, Republic of Ireland

4   TUESDAY

5   WEDNESDAY

6   THURSDAY
FULL MOON

7   FRIDAY

8   SATURDAY

9   SUNDAY

AUGUST

10 MONDAY

11 TUESDAY

12 WEDNESDAY

13 THURSDAY
LAST QUARTER

14 FRIDAY

15 SATURDAY

16 SUNDAY

AUGUST

17 MONDAY

18 TUESDAY

19 WEDNESDAY

20 THURSDAY
NEW MOON

21 FRIDAY

22 SATURDAY
First day of Ramadân (subject to sighting of the moon)

23 SUNDAY

Fenchurch Street Station welcomes Olympic visitors, 20th July 1948
Fenchurch Street Station, London, decked with banners welcoming overseas Olympic Games visitors. This station was used by the majority of visitors arriving form Tilbury Docks.

AUGUST

24 MONDAY

25 TUESDAY

26 WEDNESDAY

27 THURSDAY
FIRST QUARTER

28 FRIDAY

29 SATURDAY

30 SUNDAY

Holiday joys on the beach, 3rd September 1937

31 MONDAY
Summer Bank Holiday UK exc. Scotland

1 TUESDAY

2 WEDNESDAY

3 THURSDAY

4 FRIDAY
FULL MOON

5 SATURDAY

6 SUNDAY
Father's Day, Australia and New Zealand

SEPTEMBER

---

7 MONDAY
Holiday, USA (Labor Day)
Holiday, Canada (Labour Day)

---

8 TUESDAY

---

9 WEDNESDAY

---

10 THURSDAY

---

11 FRIDAY

12 SATURDAY
LAST QUARTER

---

13 SUNDAY

SEPTEMBER

14 MONDAY

15 TUESDAY

16 WEDNESDAY

17 THURSDAY

18 FRIDAY
NEW MOON

19 SATURDAY
Jewish New Year (Rosh Hashanah)

20 SUNDAY

Boy selling newspapers, Holyhead Station, Wales, c.1905
Official London & North Western Railway photograph showing a boy selling newspapers. The boy was employed by the newsagents WH Smith & Company to sell newspapers and magazines to passengers in the first class carriages of trains at Holyhead Station in Anglesey.

SEPTEMBER

21 MONDAY
Eid al Fitr, Ramadân ends

22 TUESDAY
Autumnal Equinox

23 WEDNESDAY

24 THURSDAY

25 FRIDAY

26 SATURDAY
FIRST QUARTER

27 SUNDAY

'Ross-on-Wye', BR (WR) poster, 1951
Poster produced for British Railways (Western Region). Artwork by Jack Merriott.

ROSS-ON-WYE

THE GATEWAY OF THE WYE

Free Guide, Chamber of Commerce, Ross-on-Wye

TRAVEL BY TRAIN

PUBLISHED BY THE RAILWAY EXECUTIVE (WESTERN REGION) (P.K. 9)

PRINTED IN GREAT BRITAIN BY JORDISON & CO. LTD. LONDON AND MIDDLESBROUGH

F.H.Glazebrook

SEPTEMBER • OCTOBER

---

28 MONDAY
Day of Atonement (Yom Kippur)

---

29 TUESDAY
Michaelmas Day

---

30 WEDNESDAY

---

1 THURSDAY

---

2 FRIDAY

---

3 SATURDAY
Festival of Tabernacles (Succoth), First Day

---

4 SUNDAY
FULL MOON

OCTOBER

---

5   MONDAY

---

6   TUESDAY

---

7   WEDNESDAY

---

8   THURSDAY

---

9   FRIDAY

---

10 SATURDAY
Festival of Tabernacles (Succoth), Eighth Day

---

11 SUNDAY
LAST QUARTER

OCTOBER

12 MONDAY
Holiday, Canada (Thanksgiving)
Holiday, USA (Columbus Day)

13 TUESDAY

14 WEDNESDAY

15 THURSDAY

16 FRIDAY

17 SATURDAY

18 SUNDAY
NEW MOON

'Royal Tunbridge Wells', BR poster, 1960
Poster produced for British Railways (BR), Southern Division to promote rail travel to Tunbridge Wells, Kent, 'Britain's Sunniest Inland Resort'.
Artwork by Johnston.

Royal
TUNBRIDGE WELLS
Britain's Sunniest Inland Resort

ONE HOUR BY TRAIN FROM LONDON AND THE SOUTH COAST
LITERATURE FROM INFORMATION BUREAU TUNBRIDGE WELLS KENT

OCTOBER

19 MONDAY

20 TUESDAY

21 WEDNESDAY

22 THURSDAY

23 FRIDAY

24 SATURDAY
United Nations Day

25 SUNDAY
British Summer Time ends

Station announcer in a loudspeaker room, 1936
Loudspeakers to announce trains first appeared at York station in 1927, and the Tannoy company introduced its products the following year. However, they were slow to catch on until after the Second World War, especially at smaller stations. In the 1930s megaphones were sometimes used, or porters shouted the arrival of trains from the platform.

OCTOBER • NOVEMBER

---

26 MONDAY
FIRST QUARTER
Holiday, New Zealand (Labour Day)
Holiday, Republic of Ireland

---

27 TUESDAY

---

28 WEDNESDAY

---

29 THURSDAY

---

30 FRIDAY

---

31 SATURDAY
Hallowe'en

---

1 SUNDAY
All Saints' Day

'Winter Sunshine', SR poster, 1932
Southern Railways posters. Artwork by JCV.

SOUTHERN
RAILWAY

WINTER
SUNSHINE

A.0.3116 1935   Sanders Phillips & Co., Ltd., THE BAYNARD PRESS, Chryssell Road, S.W.9

NORTHUM

England's most northerly county, famed for its golf

SEE BRITA

BERLAND

es and fishing streams, its castles and Roman Wall.

BY RAIL

NOVEMBER

---

2   MONDAY
FULL MOON

---

3   TUESDAY

---

4   WEDNESDAY

---

5   THURSDAY
Guy Fawkes' Day

---

6   FRIDAY

---

7   SATURDAY

---

8   SUNDAY
Remembrance Sunday, UK

Inside an ambulance train, 5th April 1918
Ambulance trains were used during the First World War in France and Belgium to transport wounded or sick soldiers to hospital. This train was on display in several stations in Lancashire and Yorkshire before being taken to the Western Front.

NOVEMBER

9 MONDAY
LAST QUARTER

10 TUESDAY

11 WEDNESDAY
Holiday, USA (Veterans Day)
Holiday, Canada (Remembrance Day)

12 THURSDAY

13 FRIDAY

14 SATURDAY

15 SUNDAY

Aldwych Station being used as an air raid shelter, c.1940
People resting and sleeping on the platform and track of Aldwych Underground Station in London during the Blitz.

NOVEMBER

LONDON MIDLAND AND SCOTTISH RAILWAY

"This is your way Sir"
IN
ENGLAND · SCOTLAND
IRELAND · WALES

16 MONDAY
NEW MOON

17 TUESDAY

18 WEDNESDAY

19 THURSDAY

20 FRIDAY

21 SATURDAY

22 SUNDAY

NOVEMBER

23 MONDAY

24 TUESDAY
FIRST QUARTER

25 WEDNESDAY

26 THURSDAY
Holiday, USA (Thanksgiving Day)

27 FRIDAY

28 SATURDAY

29 SUNDAY
First Sunday in Advent

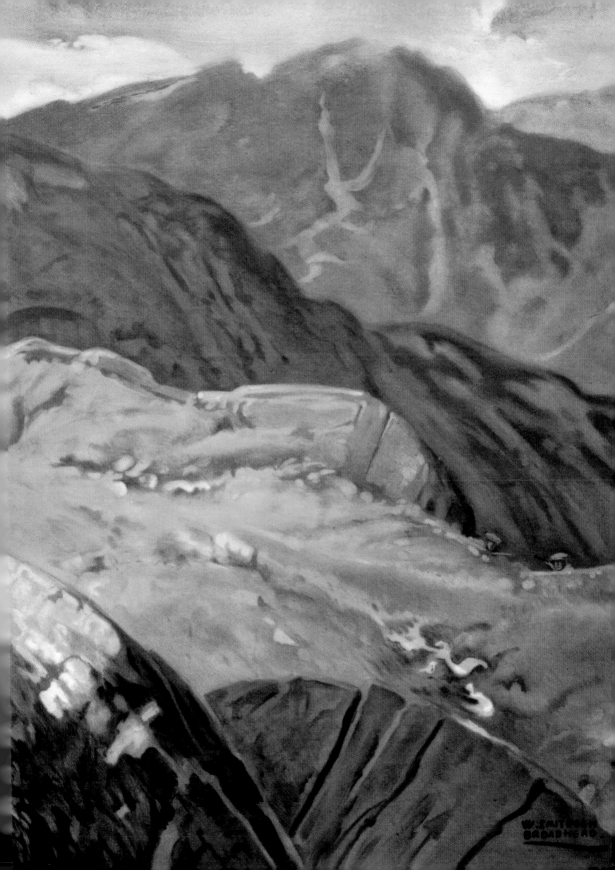

NOVEMBER • DECEMBER

---

30 MONDAY
St. Andrew's Day

---

1 TUESDAY

---

2 WEDNESDAY
FULL MOON

---

3 THURSDAY

---

4 FRIDAY

---

5 SATURDAY

---

6 SUNDAY

DECEMBER

7 MONDAY

8 TUESDAY

9 WEDNESDAY
LAST QUARTER

10 THURSDAY

11 FRIDAY

12 SATURDAY
Jewish Festival of Chanukah, First Day

13 SUNDAY

DECEMBER

---

14 MONDAY

---

15 TUESDAY

---

16 WEDNESDAY
NEW MOON

---

17 THURSDAY

---

18 FRIDAY
Islamic New Year (subject to sighting of the moon)

---

19 SATURDAY

---

20 SUNDAY

Christmas mail at King's Cross railway station, 1st December, 1960
The parcels have been unloaded from the train and are on the platform ready to be loaded into Royal Mail vans and taken to their final destinations.

DECEMBER

21 MONDAY

Winter Solstice

22 TUESDAY

23 WEDNESDAY

24 THURSDAY

FIRST QUARTER

Christmas Eve

25 FRIDAY

Christmas Day

Holiday, UK, Republic of Ireland, Canada, USA,
Australia and New Zealand

26 SATURDAY

Boxing Day (St. Stephen's Day)

27 SUNDAY

'Christmas Greetings', BR poster, 1960
Poster produced for British Railways (BR) to promote excursion and day return tickets between December 25th–27th. Artist unknown.

Christmas Greetings

SOUTHERN

173

**FOR EXCURSION AND
DAY RETURN TICKETS
FROM DECEMBER 25-27**
Ask at Stations and Travel Agents

DECEMBER • JANUARY

28 MONDAY
Holiday, UK, Canada

29 TUESDAY

30 WEDNESDAY

31 THURSDAY
FULL MOON
New Year's Eve

1 FRIDAY
New Year's Day
Holiday, UK, Republic of Ireland, Canada,
USA, Australia and New Zealand

2 SATURDAY
Holiday, Scotland and New Zealand

3 SUNDAY

Sleeping carriage, c.1930s
Sleeping carriages had been introduced in the 1870s in the luxury Pullman trains, and by 1900 sleeping cars were running between London and
Scotland, and London and the West Country.

CAPTIONS

The following captions are for the double page images:

(JAN) 'Entrance to the Locomotive Engine House, Camden Town', London, 1839. Coloured lithograph by John Cooke Bourne (1814–96), showing an engine house near Camden Town on the London & Birmingham Railway (LBR), the first railway into London. Beginning at Curzon Street Station, Birmingham, and finishing at Euston Station, London, the 112-mile long line took 20,000 men nearly 5 years to build, at a cost of five and a half million pounds. It opened on 17th September 1838; **(FEB)** 'East Coast Industries', LNER poster, c.1938. Poster produced for the London & North Eastern Railway (LNER), showing a view of St Andrew's Fish Dock, Hull, where wooden crates of fish are being unloaded from trawlers moored at the quayside. Artwork by Frank H Mason (1876–1965); **(MAR)** 'Kent – The Garden of England', BR poster, 1955. Poster produced for British Railways (BR) Southern Region (SR) to promote rail travel to the county of Kent, also known as the 'Garden of England'. Artwork by Frank Sherwin; **(APR)** 'Bath –The Georgian City', BR poster, 1950. Poster produced by British Railways (BR) to promote rail travel to Bath, North East Somerset. The poster shows a view of the Pump Room, part of the baths built by the Romans who were drawn to Bath, which they named '*Aquae Sulis*', because of its unique natural hot springs. In the 18th century, Bath was the most fashionable resort in England. Artwork by Claude Buckle (1905–73); **(MAY)** Clapham Junction, London, 1961. Colour print from a painting by Terence Cuneo looking down towards Clapham Junction in London; **(JUN)** 'Yorkshire', BR poster, 1950s. Poster produced for British Railways (BR) to promote rail travel to the county of Yorkshire. Artwork by Gyrth Russell; **(JUL)** 'Glorious Devon', BR poster, 1923–47. Colour poster produced for British Railways (BR) showing the Devonshire coastal village of Clovelly. The artist is Gyrth Russell; **(AUG)** 'Southport', LOR poster, 1923–47. Liverpool Overhead Railway poster promoting cheap fares via 'The Most Interesting Route'. The LOR (1893–1956) became the first electrically-worked elevated railway, the first to use an escalator, automatic signalling and a colour light system. Until its closure in 1956 the line remained independent, even from nationalisation. Artwork by Alfred Lambart; **(SEP)** 'Oxford', BR (WR) poster, 1958. British Railways poster promoting Oxford, the city of spires, showing Broad Street. Artwork by A Carr Linford; **(OCT)** 'Irish Mail: A Century of Service', BR poster, 1948. Poster produced by British Railways (BR) to mark the centenary of the Irish Mail route to Ireland via Holyhead and Don Laoghaire (Kingstown). The Irish Mail was the oldest named train in the world. In this poster, the train is shown leaving Robert Stephenson's mighty tubular bridge over the Menai Strait. Artwork by F H Glazebrook; **(NOV)** 'Northumberland', BR poster, 1948–65. British Railways poster. Artwork by Armangol; **(DEC)** 'Scotland for Holidays', LMS/LNER poster, 1923–47. 'Deer Stalking in the Highlands'; London Midland & Scottish Railway/London & North Eastern Railway poster showing stags amidst mountain scenery. Artwork by W Smithson Broadhead.

Other images:
(Week 2 and 3) A Southern Railway policeman and a porter, part of a set of sketches of railway workers, c.1940, by Helen McKie; **(Week 6)** One of a selection of early railway tickets, c.1870–1920. Queen's Road, Peckham to Bank, London; **(Week 12)** Shoe Black, Waterloo Station, December 1940. One of a series of watercolours of London's Waterloo Station during World War Two, by Helen McKie (d.1957), showing a serviceman in naval uniform, reading a newspaper, while a shoe black polishes his boots; **(Week 13)** Roof Spotter, Waterloo Station, December 1940. Watercolour by Helen McKie (d.1957); **(Week 15)** 'Take Your Dog', GWR/LMS/LNER/SR poster, c.1935 (detail). Poster produced for Great Western Railway (GWR), London, Midland & Scottish Railway (LMS), London & North Eastern Railway (LNER) and Southern Railway (SR) to promote return tickets at single rates for dogs travelling with their owners. Artwork by Mabel Gear; **(Week 19)** 'Avoid Crushing', BR poster, c.1950s (detail). Poster produced for British Railways (BR) staff to remind them to avoid overloading barrows. Artwork by Frank Newbould (1887–1951); **(Week 25)** A series of watercolours of London's Waterloo Station during World War Two by Helen McKie (d. 1957), **(top)** Servicewoman with a female porter, who is pushing her luggage on a trolley. The porter is wearing the uniform of the Southern Railway company. **(middle)** Policewoman conversing with a Grenadier Guard. A female porter is seen pushing a trolley full of luggage, in the background. **(bottom)** Female ticket collector in Southern Railways uniform, collecting tickets from two servicemen and one male civilian. The soldier at the front of the queue has a luggage bag with his name and regiment (East Surrey) written on it; **(Week 28)** 'Be Budget Wise!', BR poster, 1960. Poster produced for British Railways (BR) to promote budget tickets to London for shopping trips. The tickets were available on Wednesdays and Thursdays after 9.30 a.m and passengers had to depart London by 4.30 in the afternoon. Artist unknown; **(Week 33)** A selection of early railway tickets, c.1870–1920; **(Week 37)** 'Sunny South Sam', SR poster, 1939. Sunny South Sam made his debut in 1930 and quickly became a popular figure. He appeared in a variety of guises and often displayed Meteorological Office sunshine records for the South Coast resorts. Artwork by William Ramsden Brealey; **(Week 41 and Week 50)** Three model figures of railwaymen, (scale 1:4). A Stockton & Darlington railway guard c.1860, a London and South Western railway signalman c.1892, and a North Staffordshire Railway guard c.1910–13. Produced by the artist Helen McKie (d.1957), London 1957; **(Week 47)** 'This is Your Way Sir', LMS poster, c.1925. Poster produced for the London, Midland & Scottish Railway (LMS) to promote the company's porter services in stations. Artist unknown.

Hand signals, c.1910
Staff of the Lancashire and Yorkshire Railway demonstrating hand signals. Photograph taken by a Lancashire and Yorkshire Railway official photographer.